TIME for Kids

MONEY AND FINANCE

FIELD GUIDE

by **Stephen Krensky**

PENGUIN YOUNG READERS LICENSES
An imprint of Penguin Random House LLC
1745 Broadway, New York, New York 10019

First published in the United States of America by Penguin Young Readers Licenses,
an imprint of Penguin Random House LLC, 2025

TIME for Kids © 2025 TIME USA, LLC. All Rights Reserved.

Penguin Random House values and supports copyright. Copyright fuels creativity, encourages diverse voices, promotes free speech, and creates a vibrant culture. Thank you for buying an authorized edition of this book and for complying with copyright laws by not reproducing, scanning, or distributing any part of it in any form without permission. You are supporting writers and allowing Penguin Random House to continue to publish books for every reader. Please note that no part of this book may be used or reproduced in any manner for the purpose of training artificial intelligence technologies or systems.

Visit us online at penguinrandomhouse.com.

Manufactured in China

ISBN 9780593891391   10 9 8 7 6 5 4 3 2 1 TOPL

Design by Hsiao-Pin Lin

The publisher does not have any control over and does not assume any responsibility for author or third-party websites or their content.

The authorized representative in the EU for product safety and compliance is Penguin Random House Ireland, Morrison Chambers, 32 Nassau Street, Dublin D02 YH68, Ireland, https://eu-contact.penguin.ie.

. . . .

Photo credits: Cover: Getty Images: (credit card) A Mokhtari/DigitalVision Vectors; (dollars) seamartini/iStock; (finance icons) 13ree_design/iStock; (phone) simplehappyart/iStock; (piggy bank) Sammy/iStock; (wallet) Roman Bykhalets/iStock. **Interior: Adobe Stock:** icons used throughout: (business) lanastace, (credit score) IconArt, (cryptocurrency) SMUX, (finance) valeriyakozoriz, (health savings account) santricon, (income) Abbasy Kautsar, (investment) kornkun, (logistics) rtnazu, (money) Comauthor, (shopping) santricon, (thought bubble) blankstock, (volunteering) iiierlok_xolms; 5: Romolo Tavani; 6: Greatbass.com; 15: hedgehog94; 17: Marina Zlochin; 18: (face) Pattern_Repeat, (paper) warmworld; 37: MaryDesy; 46: Design Ful; 59: Flatman vector 24; 61: Drazen; 68: Uniconlabs; 82: HaRsH; 84: sudowoodo; 91: vchalup; 93: Irina Strelnikova; 97: klavdiyav. **Getty Images:** Endpapers: HADIIA POLIASHENKO/iStock; 1: Sammy/iStock; 8: filo/DigitalVision Vectors; 9, 14: Hanna Plonsak/iStock; 10: veerasakpiyawatanakul/iStock; 12: alfexe/iStock; 26: kwanchaichaiudom/iStock; 28: bortonia/DigitalVision Vectors; 39: Drazen_/E+; 40: sergeyryzhov/iStock; 42: Roman Bykhalets/iStock; 44: ArtistGNDphotography/E+; 55: Dusan Stankovic/E+; 56: Hispanolistic/E+; 58: Roman Bykhalets/iStock; 62: Nadija Pavlovic/E+; 65: mihailomilovanovic/E+; 66: LanaStock/iStock; 70: Rasi Bhadramani/iStock; 75: FreshSplash/E+; 80: da-kuk/E+; 83: Cemile Bingol/DigitalVision Vectors; 88: FilippoBacci/E+; 98: Khosrork/iStock; 100: bortonia/DigitalVision Vectors; 101: MarsBars/E+.

CONTENTS

- **04** Introduction
- **12** Earning Money
- **26** Saving Money
- **40** Spending Money
- **56** Credit
- **66** Investing
- **80** Cryptocurrency
- **88** Giving Back
- **98** Go Forth!

INTRODUCTION

Money, money, money.
   Some people think it can buy happiness. Others think it causes problems. But no matter who you are, whether you're old or young or somewhere in between, money is everywhere you look. It influences where we live, what we wear, what we eat, where we go, and how we spend our time.

All over the world, money is mostly made of coins or rectangular pieces of paper decorated with images of historical men and women. Money is also represented in the value of goods, property, and companies. Business stocks, bonds, cryptocurrencies, valuable metals like gold and silver, sparkling gems, and rare antiques all have monetary value.

Still, as common as money is now, it didn't always exist. After all, human beings have been around for a few hundred thousand years. For a long time, they had no money. Why? They didn't need it. People were far too busy just trying to survive. During the day, they hunted for animals and plants

to eat. At night, they tried to stay warm, either inside a cave or outside under the stars. When the next day dawned, they repeated the process. Under the circumstances, fire was useful. Stone tools came in handy. A successful hunt was ideal. But the biggest pile of money in the world would have been completely useless.

So, what changed? For one thing, about eleven thousand years ago, people started domesticating, or taming, animals. Raising herds of cows and flocks of sheep was a more reliable way to get food than constantly hunting wild animals. At the same time, the first farmers began growing plants near where they lived instead of roaming around picking up edible plants here and there.

Once farmers began growing more food than they needed for themselves, they had to decide what to do with the leftovers. Anyone raising animals was faced with the same question. At the same time, there were people who perhaps weren't so good at hunting or growing but had other valuable skills. Maybe they could create metal tools, skillfully cut wood, or weave useful fabrics.

Nobody today knows for sure who should get credit for what happened next, but it was a big deal. The people with extra food who lacked other valuable skills started trading with the hungry people who had valuable skills but no food. The same thing happened with the people who had animals to spare.

This was the world's first barter system: a way of directly trading one kind of thing for another. But for bartering to be successful, people on both sides had to agree on what different things were worth. Would a carpenter build a whole house in return for just one cow? Or would one cow buy only a shed? Maybe it would take five cows to pay for a whole house? Whatever the cost was going to be, both sides had to agree on it.

Early bartering systems worked well as long as everyone involved lived near one another, and as long as the only things being bartered back and forth were simple and easy to move. But what if civilization got more complicated? (It did.) What if multiple people wanted to trade a bunch of things among themselves? (They did.) Or what if someone wanted to take some of their possessions and move them from one place to another? (People did.)

To do all of this, a more flexible system was needed. It had to involve something that everyone could agree was valuable. It also had to be portable. And that's when

physical money—something people could hold in their hands and swap with one another—was invented.

One early kind of metal money was the Mesopotamian shekel, created around five thousand years ago in the Middle East. The first paper money, a banknote, came later, in the Chinese Tang dynasty in the seventh century CE. (The English word *money* first appeared in the 1300s.)

> This book includes several activities that will require you to write down your money goals and other information. Keep a pen or pencil handy so that you'll be ready to do these activities as they come up.

As more and more people began to travel over greater distances, new ways of moving and storing money appeared. Merchants from Italian city-states in the 1400s began importing and exporting goods from far away. That meant they could receive items that came from other countries and send items to other countries that came from nearby. They established banks, some of which are still operating today, to help move these transactions along. Since then, the use of money has exploded around the

INTRODUCTION | 9

world. This book will be an introduction to many of the ways you can think about money—how to earn it, save it, invest it, and how to spend it, too.

Money: an object, often a coin or paper bill, used to represent a measure of value.

Banks: financial institutions authorized to provide services related to loaning and storing money.

Bartering: the exchange of goods and services between two parties, where both sides are satisfied with the exchange.

Importing: the bringing of goods for sale from another place into a local environment.

Exporting: the transfer of local goods to a different place for sale there.

Financial resources: the existing supplies or properties that can be used to build or expand economic development.

CHAPTER 1
EARNING MONEY

How many kinds of jobs do you think there are in the world? Thousands? Millions? Whatever the real answer, these jobs share one thing in common: They represent a way to earn money. For many adults, having a job is a top priority. It allows them to earn money so they can pay for things they need or want.

Kids are in a different situation. As a kid, you have an important "job" that fills a large part of your time: your education. But you likely have other commitments—such as chores, family responsibilities, sports teams, music, and whatever else you choose or need to do. Plus, don't forget about spending time with friends. That's important, too.

As you get older, you may want to earn some money for yourself.

So, what's the best way to start making money?

Any paid job you take on has to be a part-time job because, as a student, your free time is limited. To apply for most jobs, you must be fourteen years old. However, there are certain special jobs that can be done at any age such as delivering newspapers, babysitting, and performing small chores around people's households (raking leaves, taking out the trash, walking dogs, etc.). First, think about what kind of job you'd like to do. Then, think about which job will fit your schedule. You don't have to think big at first. Even a job that only takes up a few hours here and there can be a good start.

Jobs relating to pets are one possibility. They can range from a regular position, such as walking a dog every day, to

EARNING MONEY | 15

an occasional job, like taking care of a neighbor's pets (such as dogs, cats, and fish) while they are away from home.

Household chores such as lawn mowing, snow shoveling, or car washing are also worth exploring. If these are the types of jobs you'd like to do, ask a parent or other trusted adult to help you reach out to friends and neighbors.

Being a parent's helper is another job option. Even if you are too young to babysit on your own, you may be able to help out in a household that needs an extra pair of hands while the parents are at home but busy with work or other responsibilities.

Are you especially good at math, science, a language, or another school subject? If so, you may be able to offer tutoring lessons to students who need a little extra help. You might start by tutoring students in the grades you've already completed since you'll have a good understanding of the material. A first-grade student has a lot to learn from a third-grade student!

Whatever you choose to pursue, don't think of earning money as a chore that you have to do. Instead, make it something you *want* to do! The best way to do this is to combine an interest you already have with a job. In a personal essay in the *New Yorker*, actor/comedian Amy Poehler described an early job she had serving food and cleaning up in a local restaurant. A lot of her time was spent doing physically demanding work, but "there was a performance element to the job that I found appealing . . . Every time a customer was celebrating a birthday, an employee had to bang a drum that hung from the ceiling, and play the kazoo, and encourage the entire restaurant to join him or her in a sing-along." At such times, Poehler discovered that she enjoyed making people laugh. This discovery led to a successful career making money as a comedian.

> A summer job, as the name suggests, is a job available during the summer. Unlike jobs during the school year, which are limited to hours after school or on weekends, a summer job may be full-time. It can fill up eight hours a day, five days a week. Examples of summer jobs for young people include yard work, housecleaning, camp counseling, or working at a grocery store.
>
> These jobs may not provide a weekly salary or paycheck that matches up with an hourly rate of pay, but they can still be a good way to earn money.

Imagine a fictional kid named Jack. He lives in a busy neighborhood with a mixture of individual houses and apartment buildings. He starts by thinking carefully about which jobs might fit his schedule. In addition to attending school, Jack plays sports every season, and practice sessions and games fill his weekday afternoons. But he still has some time before dinner and a lot more time on weekends.

Just because Jack is ready to work doesn't mean anyone else knows this. So, with permission and the help of a grown-up, Jack creates a flyer. It looks like this:

> Fifth grader available for odd jobs weekday afternoons before dinner and all day on weekends. I love spending time with my dog, taking care of animals, and being outdoors. Contact my parents for more information.

With his parents' help, Jack spreads the word to neighbors and nearby friends. Over the next few days, he gets several replies. One is from his next-door neighbor.

She works late on Thursdays and needs someone to walk her dog just before six. Jack realizes he can fit this job in after sports, but before having dinner at home.

Another neighbor reaches out to Jack's dad. He is looking for someone to mow his small backyard once a week. This neighbor owns a lawn mower, which Jack can use. He knows he can easily find time to mow each weekend. So Jack now has two ways to regularly make some money.

Finding a part-time job may be as simple as that. Or it may be more complicated depending on where you live and which jobs are available near you. But you can only find out which jobs actually exist by exploring your options. So get out there and see what happens!

Activity 1

Make a list of eight different jobs you think you could do now. Circle your three top choices. Why do you think those would be the best options for you? Explain your thinking.

_____

_____

_____

_____

_____

_____

_____

Activity 2

Do you have a dream job in mind for when you grow up? It could be anything—an astronaut, a marine biologist, a doctor, a plumber. Ideally, you pick a job that matches your skills, interests, and financial needs. There's an old saying that goes, "Find a job you love, and you'll never work a day in your life."

_____

_____

_____

Can you find out more about this dream job? Do some research at your local library. What kind of education does it require? What would you do in that job every day? Is this a routine you can get excited about? How much money will you earn?

Your Hot Job

Are you curious to discover your own dream job? It's completely normal to not have one in mind just yet! A world of **career** options awaits. **Your Hot Job** is a program designed by TIME for Kids that empowers kids ages eight to fourteen to find their future on a path that's just right for them. Visit **www.timeforkids.com/your-hot-job/** to take the Skills Explorer quiz and earn badges as you explore exciting careers.

Salary: a fixed amount of money an employee earns for a specific job measured over the course of one year.

Hourly rate: the amount an employee earns each hour for the work performed.

Paycheck: an amount paid to an employee on a regular basis (weekly, biweekly, or monthly) in return for work performed.

CHAPTER 2
SAVING MONEY

Once you earn some money, you will have to make an important decision. What should you do with it? You may be tempted to spend all your money as quickly as you make it. And if you do that, you won't ever have to figure out what to do with your savings—because you won't have any! But if you choose to spend every dollar you earn, you may miss out on bigger opportunities down the road.

Saving money is about establishing a financial goal and figuring out a way to reach it. First, you have to decide what you're saving for. Is it for emergencies or for a specific item like a video game? Second, do you have a limited amount of time to earn the money for the item or experience you are saving for? You'll have to pay close attention to that. Third, is there a way you can measure your progress as your savings begin to build? As you get closer to reaching your goal, make sure to give yourself credit for what you're accomplishing.

Founding Father Benjamin Franklin once said, "If you would be wealthy, think of saving as well as getting."

What did he mean by this? Franklin was making the point that saving money is just as important as earning money in the journey to becoming financially successful. Obviously he understood that people may need to spend money on necessary things such as food or shelter. If your responsibilities include contributing money to your family's daily life, of course they come first. Franklin is simply saying that making sure to save the money that you *can* save is very important. There is a big difference between the things you *want* to spend money on and the things you *need* to spend money on.

Understanding this difference is key. Imagine the case of Emily, a fifth grader whose mother gives her $5 to pay for lunch at school. But what if on the way to school, she passes a toy store with a glow-in-the-dark yo-yo on sale for just $5? Emily really wants the yo-yo, but if she buys it, she'll have nothing left over for lunch. The yo-yo is a want, while lunch is a need.

That doesn't mean that ongoing needs never leave room for anything else. Saving money should come with a little bit of flexibility. It's perfectly fine sometimes to spend money on a treat. There also isn't one single rule that can guide you about saving. There may be a special event that you want to save money for, like tickets to a concert. Or you may want to put away enough money to pay for gifts for others around the holidays.

Figuring all that out is why it's a good idea to make a budget. Once you make a list of your expenses, you can measure that against the money you're earning. Aditi, for example, wants to buy a bicycle for $400. She starts out with $120 that she has saved. That leaves her needing another $280. Every week, she earns $40 doing chores at her family's hardware store. If Aditi saves all of that, seven weeks later, she will have enough to buy her bike. However, if she saves only $20 each week and spends the other $20 on other things, then it will take twice as long—fourteen weeks—to reach her goal.

Saving money doesn't mean you have to start out by saving big. Big or small, the secret to successful saving is to do it regularly. If you start a part-time job, you should sit down with an adult to figure out what you should do with the money you're earning. It could be the best course of action to divide the money into pieces for saving or spending. Of course, saving could be just for a short period of time, or it could be toward something really big further off in the future, like going to college. (And in that case, you're going to want to put the money in a savings account where it can earn interest while it grows.)

Benjamin Franklin accomplished a lot of things in his life. He was a printer, an inventor, a politician, a statesman, a scientist, and a philosopher. Franklin was known for believing that saving money whenever one is able to—even if it is just a penny—is incredibly important. Now, even in Franklin's time, the 1700s, a penny was not a lot of money. But Franklin's point was simple. Any penny you save for later use is a penny you won't have to earn later. And even though each penny doesn't seem like much on its own, those pennies taken together can really add up.

Even if you don't have a bigger purchase in mind right now, saving your money for later use is always a good idea.

Activity 3

• • •

Think of three things that you would like to have. How much does each of them cost? How much do all three items cost together? How much money do you currently have? How much money do you still have to save for all three things? What can you do to reach that goal amount? How long will it take?

_____

_____

_____

_____

_____

_____

Activity 4

• • •

Interview an adult about what "needs" are necessary to budget for each month. This might be groceries, rent or mortgage payments, gas, and clothing. Are there any items on the list that surprise you?

_____

_____

_____

_____

_____

_____

_____

SAVING MONEY | 35

SAVING MONEY | 37

Budget: a spending plan covering a specific period of time. It measures income against expenses in the hope that the income will be greater than the expenses.

Interest: a yearly percentage of money connected to a loan or savings. For a loan, it is the additional amount of money the borrower must pay while the loan is in effect. If the interest is connected to a savings account, it is the extra money a bank has agreed to pay the account owner in return for leaving the money in that account.

Savings account: a type of bank account that stores money and usually pays a small amount of interest.

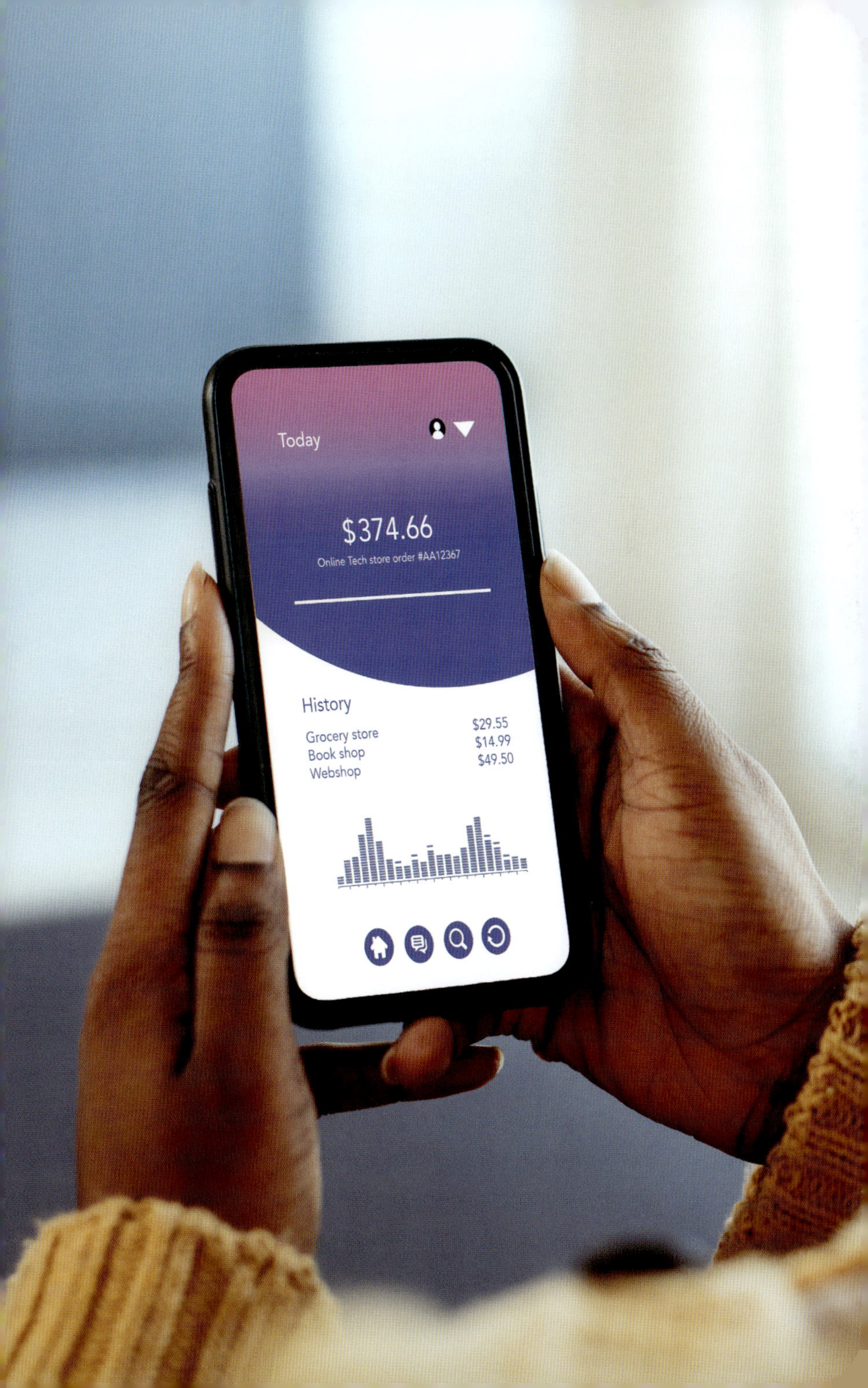
Today
$374.66
Online Tech store order #AA12367
History
Grocery store
Book shop
Webshop
$29.55
$14.99
$49.50

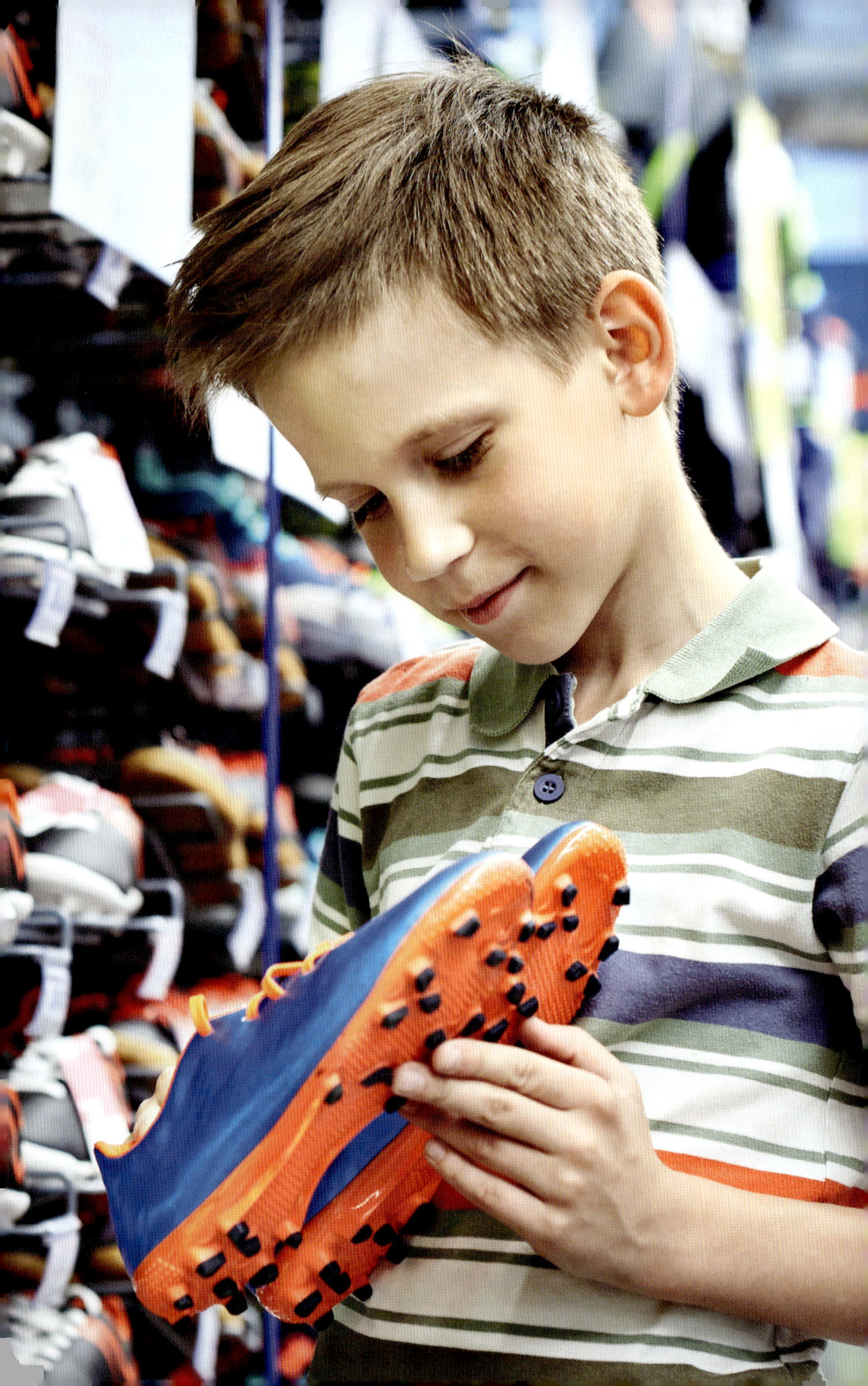

CHAPTER 3
SPENDING MONEY

Spending money can take you in a lot of different directions. You could be making an "impulse purchase" you didn't plan for in advance. Or you could be meeting a financial goal—maybe fulfilling a longtime dream.

Imagine that Obi starts the new school year by spending all of his savings on a pair of sneakers he spots in a store. At that moment, it seemed like a good idea because he had the money and liked the sneakers. But Obi's current sneakers still fit him and he didn't need new shoes. A few weeks later, Obi realizes he shouldn't have spent all his money on sneakers because he has nothing left to buy his sister Aisha a birthday present. He can still make her a card, but he knows Aisha will have some hurt feelings.

So when it comes to spending money, it's good to think ahead. And that means doing more than just figuring out what to spend your money on. You should also pay attention to where and when you spend the money. How do you do that? By being a smart shopper.

> In the summer of 2019, Popeyes, the fried chicken chain, introduced a fried chicken sandwich. At the time, Popeyes had planned ahead enough by ordering ingredients for the sandwich that would last through September. However, the sandwich was so popular, Popeyes ran out of the ingredients by the end of August. It took months for Popeyes to figure out the right formula for buying the ingredients to match the speed of their sandwich sales.

Timing can make a difference. For example, if you buy a new video game the week it comes out, you'll pay the highest price. If you can be patient, the price may come down over time as the demand—the number of people desperate to buy a product—for the new game eases up. Prices of almost everything are influenced by the tug-of-war between supply and demand.

There are other ways to be a savvy shopper. Sales are often tied to holidays like Labor Day or Presidents' Day. Beyond those, there are also some well-known annual sales like Black Friday, the Friday after Thanksgiving. Black Friday has become famous as a date when stores offer their lowest prices of the year.

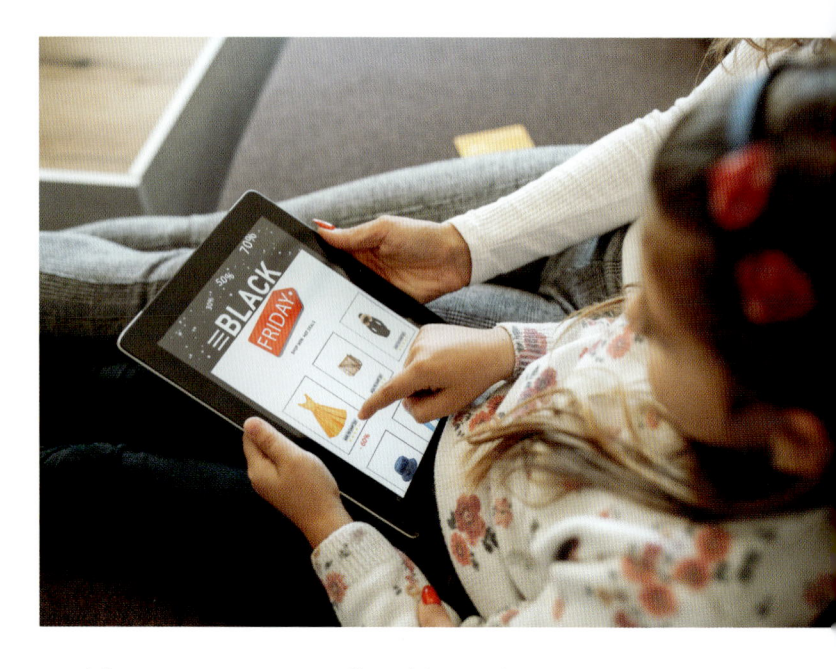

These savings can really add up. If you save $20 on a pair of jeans that normally costs $50, that's 40 percent off, which is a lot. If you save $100 on a computer tablet that normally costs $400, that's only 25 percent less, but the savings are bigger because the starting price was higher. Searching for sales may sometimes feel a little boring, but just remember how many hours it takes to earn the money you'll be saving. It's also important to remember that you should not just spend money at sales for the sake of shopping—you should look out for sales on items you truly need or have wanted for a long time.

Another way to spend money wisely on purchases is to use discount coupons. Sometimes, the coupons are for a specific amount, like $5 off a particular item in a specific store. Other times the coupon is for some percent of the price, such as 20 percent off. In that case, the higher the cost, the bigger the discount.

Another thing to consider when spending money is the quality of what you're buying. There's an old saying that "you get what you pay for." What does this mean? If something has a low price, it may be because it is not made as well as a more expensive version of the same item. Before you spend your money, it's a good idea to do some research, read reviews, and then decide which item to buy.

Olivia is looking to buy some earbuds. She looks online and finds two pairs that look the same. One costs $39.99, and the other is $69.99. The $39.99 pair is from a company she has never heard of. The more expensive pair is from a well-known brand. Olivia listens to both pairs in a store, and to her ears, they sound about the same. But when Olivia reads some online reviews, alarm bells go off. The brand-name pair is well regarded, consistently getting good reviews. The less expensive earbuds, though, have drawn a lot of complaints. Apparently the earbuds break quickly, in just a month or two. If the cheaper earbuds don't last, they won't turn out to have been a bargain because Olivia will just have to buy another pair and spend even more money. So after studying the pros and cons, Olivia decides to save

When you're thinking about buying something, it makes sense to find a review of the product. With an adult's help, you can search for a video review online. It will explain what the product is and how it works. Whoever is doing the demonstration may be really enthusiastic about sharing the product with you. But be careful. Is the person giving the review doing it because they actually care about and like the product? Sometimes that person is being paid by the company that makes the product to say favorable things about it. You need to find out what's really going on before relying on the review to influence your decision. Look for words like "sponsored" or "ad." These can be clues.

up for the more expensive pair. She decides they will be a better purchase in the long run.

Sometimes, however, the cheaper product does the job just as well as the expensive version. Mei wants to buy a new backpack for school because she outgrew her old one. She decides that she wants a pink one. She has a budget of $25. At the store, there are two pink backpacks. One is $19.99 and the other is $54.99. The only difference between the two backpacks is that the more expensive one is from a well-known brand while the cheaper one is not. When Mei looks at reviews online, she sees that buyers are very happy with the quality of the cheaper option. She buys that one and is able to stay within her budget while getting what she wanted: a pink backpack.

Here's another truth about money: Sometimes spending money now can help you save money in the future. If you have a bicycle, you may want to keep the item in good shape by getting it oiled and cleaned every year. Sure, this will cost some money now, but keeping a bicycle working well will make it last longer. If you don't take care of your bike, you may have to replace it sooner. And buying a brand-new bike will cost a lot more than oiling and cleaning your current bike once a year.

Activity 5

What is the most memorable thing you've ever spent money on? What made this purchase so special? Was it something that you used for a long time, or was it something that only briefly fit your needs?

_____

_____

_____

_____

_____

_____

_____

_____

SPENDING MONEY | 49

Activity 6

Think of a food you really like. With a parent's help, go online to look up what it costs at different stores near where you live, or go there to check. Is the price of that food the same everywhere? Is it more expensive at one type of store than it is at another? If so, why do you think this is?

_____

_____

_____

_____

_____

_____

Activity 7

Imagine you're at the grocery store and you want to buy a candy bar. How can you be sure that you're getting the best deal on the sweet treat you want? It's not always as simple as picking the chocolate bar with the lowest price. Sometimes, lower prices mean smaller portions, so you're actually paying more for less product. This is why it's important to compare prices.

Comparing prices, or comparison shopping, involves putting one item next to a similar item to figure out which one gives you more for your money. Because of the way things are packaged, this isn't always easy. To figure out the better deal, check the unit price. It lets you see how much one measure of an item—like an ounce of candy—will cost you, so you can compare apples to apples.

Often, stores show the unit price right on the shelf. If they don't, you can calculate it yourself. In a store, you might see a bag of candy that has 50 pieces for $6.99 right next to a bag that has 80 pieces of the same candy—same brand, same size—for $11.99. It's easy to think, "Bigger bag, better deal." But is that really true? You can calculate a unit price—in this case, a single piece of candy—to find out. Here's how: Take the total price of a bag and divide it by the number of pieces.

[PRICE OF BAG] ÷ [NUMBER OF PIECES] = [PRICE PER PIECE]

Go to a grocery store near you and head to the candy aisle. Pick two similar bags of candy and compare which one is a better deal per piece by doing the math above!

Supply: the currently available stock of products or items available for purchase

Demand: the desire in the marketplace for a particular item. When the demand is greater than the supply, the item will become unavailable.

SPENDING MONEY | 55

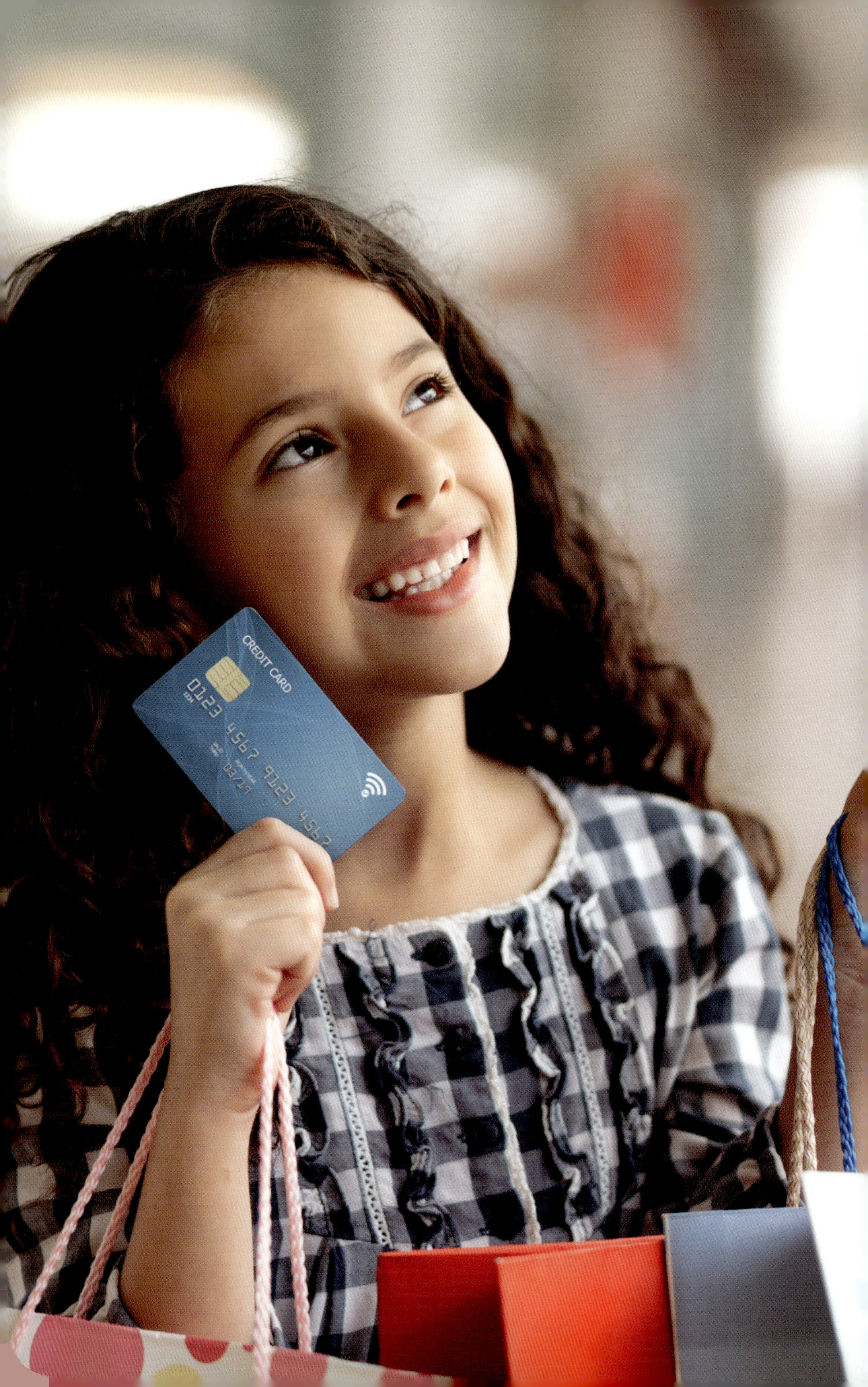
CREDIT CARD
0123
4567 9123 4567

CHAPTER 4
CREDIT

Credit is the ability to buy something now and pay for it later. Why do people choose to do this? That's simple. Because they want to buy something before they have saved up all the money they need to purchase it.

The most common form of credit comes from using credit cards. To get a credit card, adults must first apply to a bank and agree they will pay back any money they borrow. Once you have a credit card, you can use it to purchase anything you would pay for with cash, like clothing, groceries, gas, furniture, meals, or toys. When paying with a credit card, though, you don't have to give the store the money when you take home the item. Instead, you promise to pay for it later, when the bill arrives.

After a few weeks, the credit card company sends you a bill, which lists all the items you've purchased using your card. If you have the money to pay back the whole amount you borrowed when the bill arrives, then you can do that, and there is no charge for the credit card company's service. But if you don't have enough money to pay the entire amount when the monthly bill arrives, you can pay a smaller amount. In return for this benefit, though, you will start paying interest—a fee that is a percentage of the money you still owe.

So, is using a credit card a good idea?

Let's say Rikki plays electric guitar in a band, and her guitar is damaged in an accident. A new guitar will cost $300. Rikki needs the new guitar right away because without it, she can't play in the band. (And if she's not playing in a band, she's not making any money.) Rikki can afford to spend $80 each month toward a new guitar, but she

There's an ongoing debate about which school grade is the right one to introduce students to the principles of personal finance. Some educators and students believe an early introduction will have a better chance of taking root and leading students in a responsible direction. Others believe that elementary and middle schools should be focusing on reading, math, and critical thinking skills, and there's plenty of time to have students develop financial literacy later. The solution may lie somewhere in the middle, where financial topics are used as examples to anchor more basic educational skills. What do you think?

doesn't have enough to buy it outright today.

Rikki has already figured out that if she buys the new $300 electric guitar now on a credit card and pays 14 percent interest, she will pay a little more than $8 altogether in interest—as long as she pays off the debt in four months, which is possible because of the money she earns from playing in the band. Of course, it's always better to pay no interest, but $8 in interest is a manageable expense if it allows Rikki to buy the guitar and keep earning money playing in her band.

Another kind of card that looks like a credit card but operates differently is a debit card. This card is tied directly to your checking account, a type of bank account that allows you to quickly pay for regular purchases with money you have at a bank. You can use a debit card instead of writing a check or withdrawing your cash from your bank in person. And unlike a credit card, debit cards won't charge interest. Debit cards work in stores, as well as at ATMs (automated teller machines) if you simply want to get some cash without going inside a bank.

But be careful! A debit card can be costly if you take out more money than your account holds. You might assume that a bank will simply reject your request to get money from an ATM if your account is empty. But this is not true. Many banks will give you the extra money anyway. Why? Because they will charge you a stiff penalty for the convenience. So, unless you're in a real emergency, be sure you have enough money in your account before you use a debit card.

It's important to be very careful about taking on credit-related debt. But in some cases, like when paying for education or financing a car or a home, taking on credit is a common option. To finance a house loan, a bank gives the buyer a mortgage. This is an agreement—a contract—between the bank and the borrower that states that the borrower will pay back the loan with interest over a certain number of years. And what happens if the borrower stops paying? In that case, the bank can legally step in and take the house back. So clearly, people buying a home must make sure they can afford to pay back the loan over the time agreed on.

Another thing that happens as you buy things with credit is the building of your credit score. These scores come from companies that keep track of all the money you borrow and how quickly you pay it back. If you always make payments on time, you get a good rating. But if you skip payments or fall behind, your rating will drop. Why does this matter? Your credit rating follows you around no matter where you go. Later on, when you may be making a big purchase like a car or a house, a higher rating will get you a better interest rate on your loan. But don't worry if you make some mistakes early on. Your personal score can improve over time as you build a better credit history in the future.

Credit card: a thin, rectangular piece of plastic issued by a bank or financial services company. It allows a cardholder to charge items and then pay for these items later, either all at once or gradually over a longer period of time.

Credit score: a number that evaluates an individual person's credit risk based on that person's overall financial history.

Debit card: a card linked to a bank checking account that allows the owner to withdraw money from that account to pay for purchases directly.

Credit limit: the maximum amount of money the owner of the card is allowed to borrow. This limit can range from a few hundred dollars for new cardholders to many thousands of dollars for experienced borrowers.

Debt: any amount of money owed by one person to another person or a financial institution.

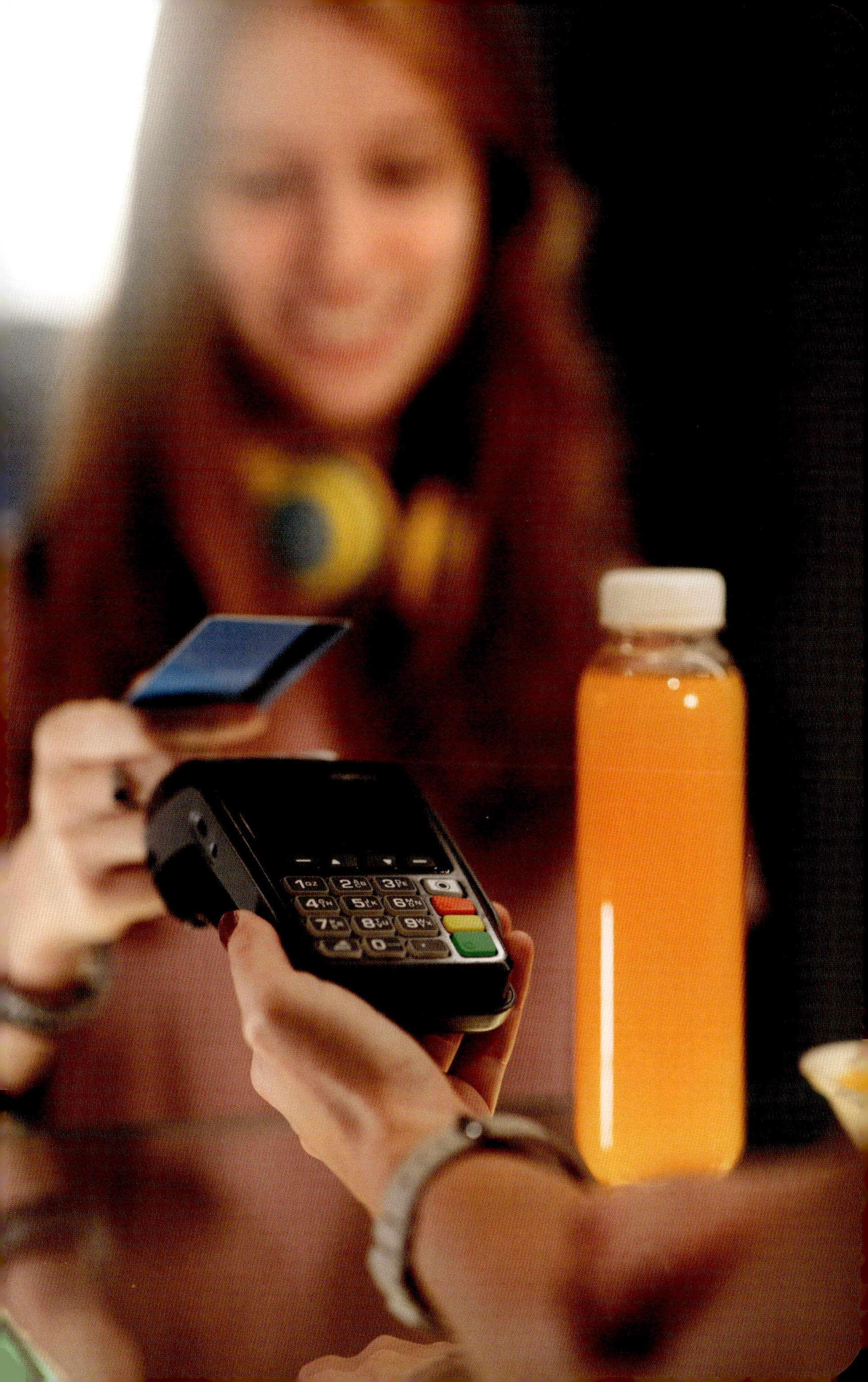

15,7103
15,71 $ -7,79 %
17,2990
15,5512
15 1 4 1
(7):16,7697
(25):14,0054
(99):8,6236
19,4000
20,0000
15,7103
15,0000
10,0000
8 269 671,65
12-16
12-28
01-09
01-21
0.0001

CHAPTER 5
INVESTING

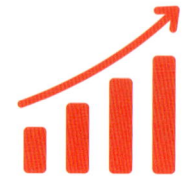

What does it mean to make an investment? It means that you are looking to grow your money by putting a portion of it in a place where it can expand into a higher amount. If possible, it's good to have that money earn some kind of return until you need it. An investment may be a stock, a bond, a piece of property, or something else.

This growth is what separates investing from saving. If you put $100 in a bank, and it pays an interest rate of 2 percent a year, then you will earn $2 a year in interest. In contrast, for decades, people who invest in the stock market have earned interest of about 10 percent a year. So $100 invested there could earn $10 a year, five times as much as a bank may offer.

The first national bank in the United States opened in 1791. For a very long time, people have put their money in banks because they are seen as a safe place to keep money. Banks also offer some interest in return for holding your deposit. Today, any money you deposit in an account at an approved American bank is protected by the United States government. (There is a limit of $250,000 for each depositor in one bank, which is more than enough for most people. Anyone who has more money than that can protect it by opening more accounts at other banks.)

However, you do pay a "price" for that safety because banks will not pay very much interest to hold your money. A typical savings account holding $100 might earn only a few dollars a year.

If you want to earn more than that, you will need to take a bigger risk. Most of the time, people take that risk in the stock market. Stock exchanges are the places where shares of public companies can be bought or sold. Stock trading happens mostly online—you don't have to actually go to the stock exchange in order to buy a share! These shares are regulated by the government to make sure they are legitimate. The price of these shares varies from one company to the next. It is based on what people think the company is worth (which can change even from one minute to the next). But stock returns are in no way guaranteed. If you choose a risky investment, even one that promises a big return, you may be taking a chance that some of your original money will be lost. Typically, the bigger the return, the more risk is at stake.

So, is investing in the stock market a good idea for you? If you're planning to use the $100 to buy something soon, it may not be worth the risk of losing any of your original money while hoping to slightly increase your overall total. Even though the stock market has gone up on average for many years, there have been periods where it went down, sometimes sharply.

The American writer Mark Twain once said that there

are two times in a person's life when they should not speculate: when they can't afford it, and when they can. This means that a person should not consider buying something if they aren't sure that they have the money to buy it. Unfortunately, Twain knew all about putting money into risky ventures from his own personal experience. He lost most of his life savings jumping into one bad investment after another—telegraphs, watchmaking, railroads, and more. His big problem was his enthusiasm for taking a chance—for speculating on what he saw as a golden opportunity. Twain would get so excited about some new venture that he wouldn't study the details long enough to see if the business was truly a good investment.

Therefore, if you're thinking about investing your money in a specific company, you should first learn as much as you can about it. But which company should that be? You could start with a company that you already know, such as Nike or McDonald's or Disney. But you shouldn't choose a company just because its sneakers are cool, its burgers taste good, or even because you've seen one of its movies a million times.

In the case of Nike, for example, you will want to learn what the value of the stock is. How is it priced now compared to other times? Is it at an all-time high, an all-time low, or somewhere in between? An all-time high may

When Jaydyn Carr was six years old, his mother, Nina Carr, gave him a present. It was ten shares of GameStop stock that she bought for about $62. The gift was meant to teach *ujamaa*, one of the seven principles of Kwanzaa. "*Ujamaa* is a Swahili word meaning 'cooperative economics,'" Nina explained in an interview with *TIME for Kids*. She then had to explain to Jaydyn that he now owned a small piece of the company. This was an exciting idea, especially since GameStop was one of his favorite stores. The stock price has since risen and fallen dramatically, but it is still worth more than what Nina Carr first paid for it.

mean that Nike has figured out the market and keeps creating sneakers that leave other footwear companies in the dust. But the high stock price could also mean that the company had a very successful sneaker launch recently, but has no new models coming up to keep the momentum going. It could be helpful to research what Nike is releasing in the next few months to see if people are excited about what is coming soon. On the other hand, a low stock price might mean that a company has made decisions that caused it to lose the trust of its customers and supporters. It is important to do research before buying any stock to see how the company is growing or know about any obstacles they are facing.

One teenage investor, Noa Polish, has been a shareholder of Mondelēz since she was nine years old. Mondelēz is the company that manages, among other foods, OREO cookies and Ritz crackers. But Noa has never settled for just reading about the company in articles or annual reports. "I like listening to the CEO (chief economic officer) discuss our business," she says. And to do that, she goes to the annual meeting that is open to shareholders. "I even asked a question—I was nervous at first, but it felt great." And she has some general advice for any other young investors. "If you have a company you really like and you trust that the product is good, try investing in it."

All of this shows that making an investment is not something to do lightly. It will require your interest, time, and energy. But if you're willing to make the proper commitment, investing may enable you to make more with your money going forward.

INVESTING | 73

Investment: the placing of money in a company or organization with the hope of increasing the value of this money in a productive way.

Stock market: an organization of different companies whose shares can be bought or sold.

Stock: a small piece of ownership in a company. Many companies have millions of shares of stock that collectively represent the value of the whole company.

Bonds: documents issued by governments or companies to raise money. People invest in bonds to get a favorable interest rate in return for keeping the bond for several years.

Speculate: to think about something and make guesses about it.

Shareholder: a person who owns a small portion of a company or property.

Risk: a situation involving potential for danger or loss.

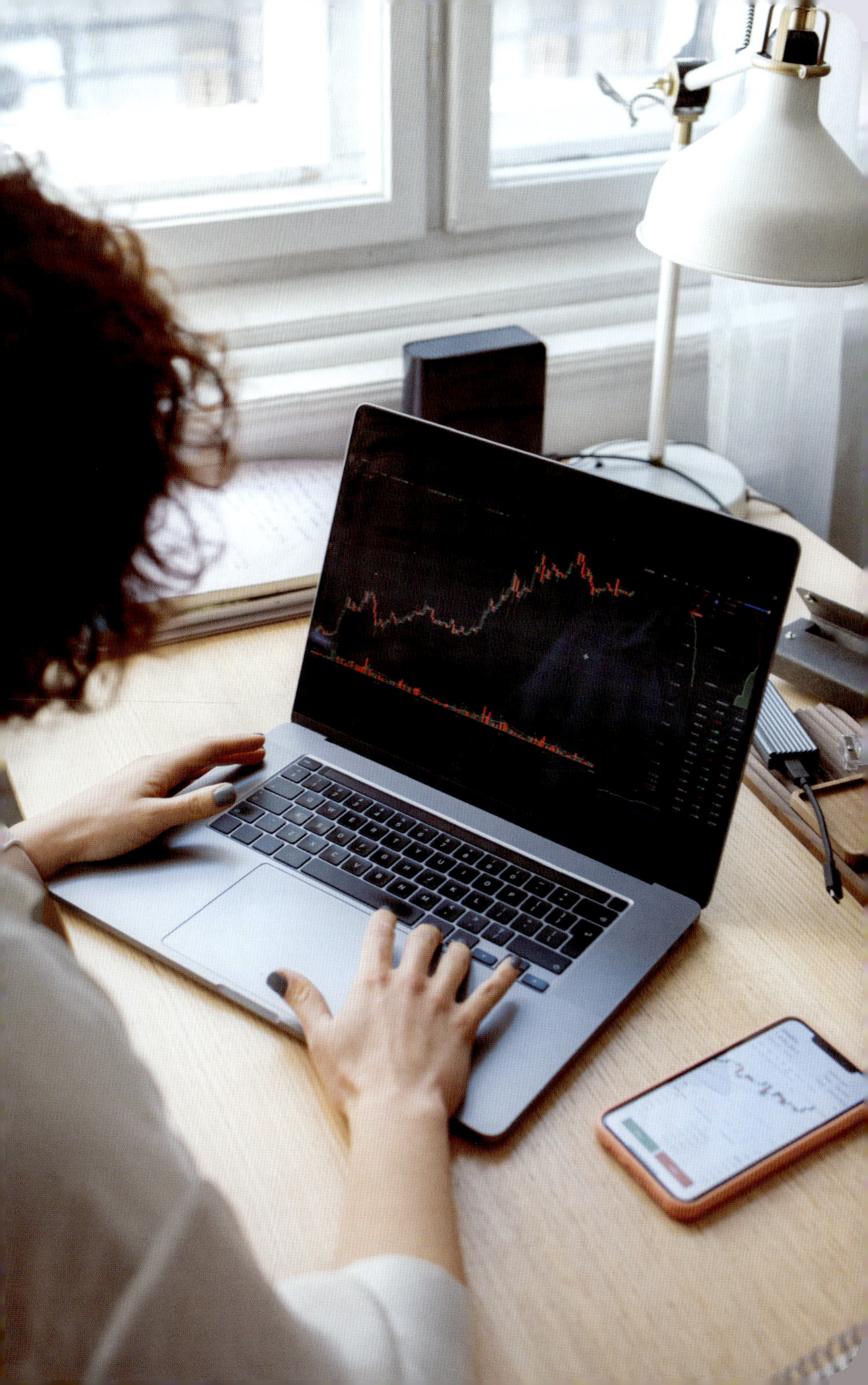

Activity 8

With an adult, do some research on a stock you might like to invest in. Think of big companies that you like, such as Netflix, Nintendo, or Mattel. How much does one share cost? Has the price gone up or down today? In the past week? In the past six months? In the past year? Does this seem like a good stock to invest in? Why or why not?

_____

_____

_____

_____

_____

Activity 9

Choose a company. Pretend you had bought ten shares of its stock a year ago today. What would that have cost you then? What would the value of those shares be today? Would this have been a good investment? Why or why not?

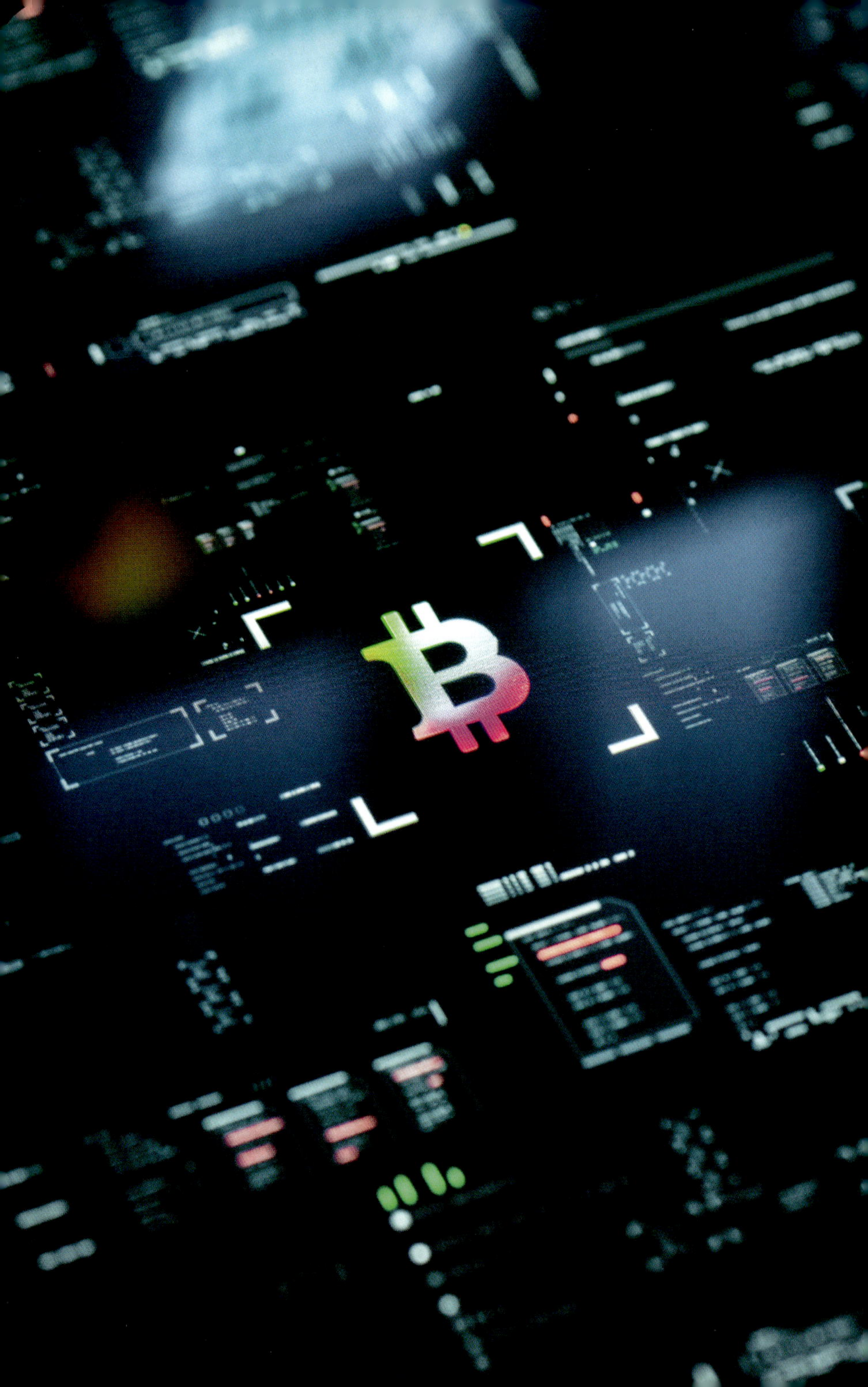

CHAPTER 6
CRYPTOCURRENCY

Everyone is very accustomed to the coins and paper money we use today. Money has changed over time; the metal in the coins and the kinds of paper may have been tweaked here and there. But the idea behind money has not changed in a very long time. And all of these different kinds of money are used in different countries. Each government supports its own currency.

This system has worked well, but it does have limitations. Years ago, the United States, like many countries, followed the "gold standard." For every dollar the American government issued, an equivalent amount of gold actually was stored in a vault. That rule no longer exists. Today, our money has value simply because the government says it does.

Other things have changed, too. In the digital age we now live in, technology doesn't stand still for long, and new ideas crop up all the time. Cryptocurrency (or "crypto" for short) is one of those ideas, and it represents a significant change in what money can be. Think about the tokens you may use when playing an online video game to buy improvements of one kind or another. You earn these tokens as you play, or you buy them with regular money. Inside the game, though, these digital tokens have a concrete value. Now, imagine that digital token could be used in the real world. Those tokens would be a form of cryptocurrency.

Unlike paper money or coins, crypto isn't something you can put in your pocket or hold in your hand. It's created with computer programs and only exists in computer files. But as unfamiliar as this sounds, crypto works like real money. There are more than one thousand cryptocurrencies in use, but Bitcoin is the best known.

Since Bitcoin isn't something you can hold, though, you can't take it to a store to buy things. To spend Bitcoin, you need a digital wallet. It works like a bank account installed on your computer or smartphone. With your digital wallet, you can spend Bitcoin at websites and stores around the world. What can it buy? Almost anything, from toys to books to much bigger things like houses.

The idea of cryptocurrency has been around for decades, but its first actual appearance is traced to 2009 when Bitcoin was introduced to the financial marketplace. Everyone understood that digital currencies like Bitcoin were not backed by banks or governments. They operated without

The first purchase made with Bitcoin was for an order of Papa John's pizza. The computer programmer Laszlo Hanyecz used 10,000 units of Bitcoin to make the purchase (about $41 at the time). This event took place on May 22, 2010, and is celebrated each year on May 22 as Bitcoin Pizza Day.

oversight. This gave them great flexibility while also making them unpredictable. Determining their value at any given moment is complicated. Therefore, they can swing wildly from day to day or even moment to moment. This makes them among the riskiest of investments. Some established financial advisers recommend staying clear of them altogether.

> Crypto enthusiasts have embraced NFTs as a new kind of investment for digital art lovers. NFT is an acronym for non-fungible token. What does non-fungible mean? It means that the thing that was bought cannot be exchanged for anything else. It is a kind of collector's item that comes with a digital certificate authenticating its value. An NFT could be digital art or music. It starts with a specific value, and like other collectibles, that value can rise or fall over time.

Cryptocurrency has value because people believe in it. A big reason for that is that all the transactions that happen on computers leave a record behind. This record is kept in a digital ledger using a technology called blockchain. This technology uses cryptography, a special code, to keep the transactions from being hacked or stolen. Blockchain also allows users to transfer money from one place in the world to another using the internet.

Even though cryptocurrencies are relatively new, there are already many stories about people who have made or lost fortunes with their crypto investments. It's a little bit like the get-rich-quick stories that circulated back around the time of the California Gold Rush in 1849. Tales of fortunes seemingly made overnight reached the East. Fear of missing out prompted thousands of people to quit their jobs, pack up their belongings, and head west as fast as possible. The truth, though, was a little less rosy. There were no guarantees involved in digging for gold, and most people failed at it miserably. The price of Bitcoin has gone up and down from a few dollars to tens of thousands of dollars. This kind of movement has prompted many experts to warn against crypto as an investment.

There are now more than twenty thousand cryptocurrencies in the world. Will they someday become as common or accepted as the paper and metal money that has been circulated for hundreds of years? That's hard to say, and many people remain skeptical of cryptocurrency and its future. However, its supporters don't get discouraged easily. They are trying very hard to earn themselves a permanent place at the financial table.

Cryptocurrency: money that exists only in digital form, not in physical form.

Bitcoin: a type of cryptocurrency.

Digital wallet: where a person stores their cryptocurrency.

Cryptography: a special code that keeps cryptocurrency transactions from being hacked or stolen.

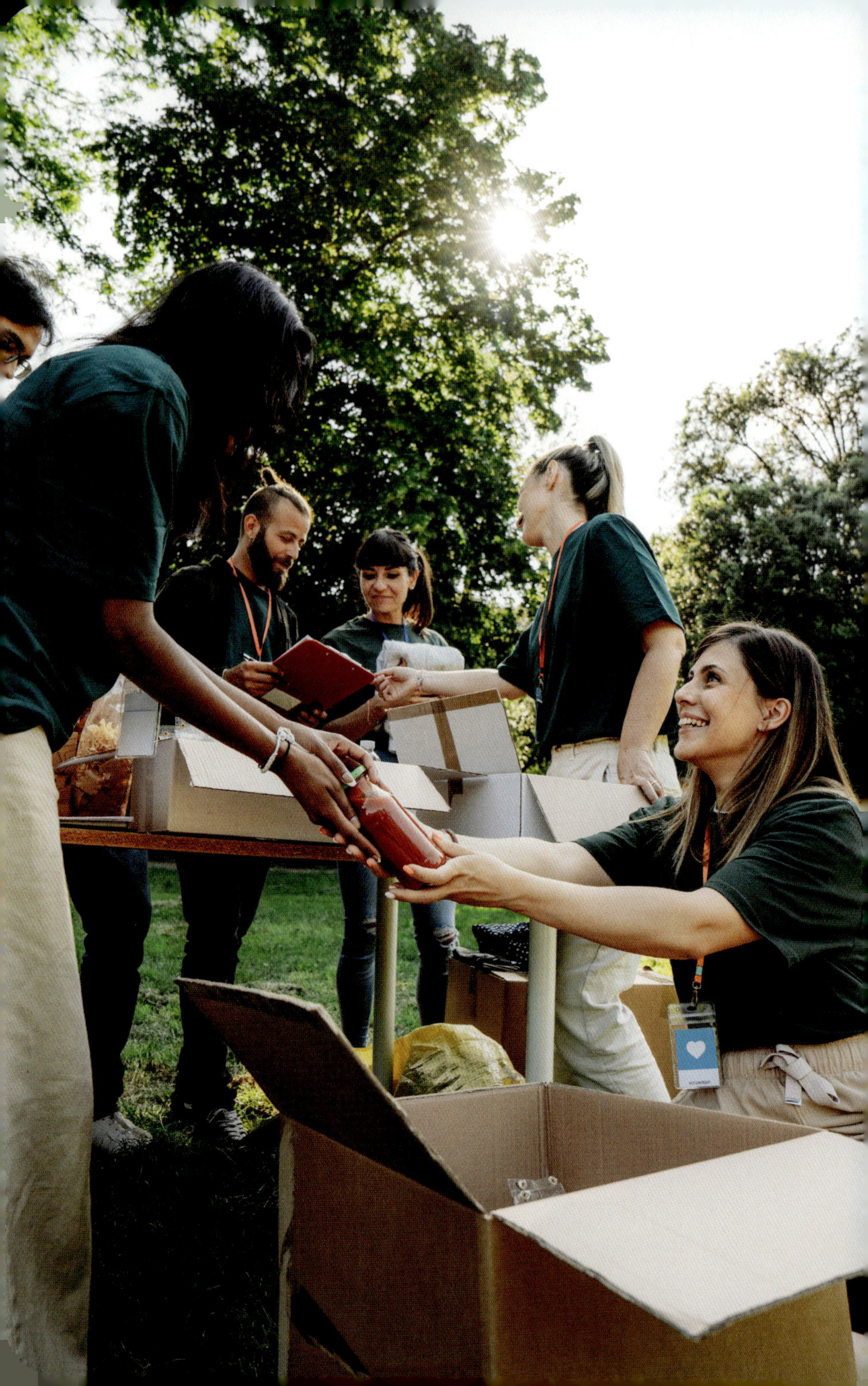

# CHAPTER 7
GIVING BACK

Earning, saving, and investing money can all be very satisfying. But there's one other special thing you can do with some of your money.

Give it away. As Lady Gaga said, "I don't want to make money. I want to make a difference."

Wealthy people have donated to charity for a long time. But the explosion of wealth at the end of the 1800s led to a new level of giving. Andrew Carnegie was a businessman who lived during the 1800s and 1900s. He was born in Scotland but made his vast fortune in the United States in the steel business. He spent millions of dollars to create more than 2,500 town libraries in the United States, Canada, and other countries around the world. More than 800 of those libraries are still in use today.

On a personal level, you already make a kind of donation when you buy a gift for a friend or a family member. But contributing to a worthy cause has a different kind of value. All kinds of nonprofit organizations exist and would welcome your contributions, big or small. Philanthropy is the act of donating money to one or more of these groups whose work you want to support.

Sometimes you may feel a personal connection to one particular organization. If you have a pet, you may want to donate to an animal shelter. Or maybe you are concerned

Teachers at Elliott Elementary in McKinney, Texas, were unable to buy new iPads and computers for their students because they didn't have enough money in the budget. So they decided to hold a fundraiser in which students would run laps around the school track in exchange for donations. For example, fourth grader Bennett Webster raised $100 from running forty-six laps. In total, the school raised $41,000 and was able to purchase the new technology it needed.

about those who don't have enough to eat on a daily basis. You might want to contribute to a local food bank, which gathers food items from the government or grocery stores and then distributes the food to people in need. Or if protecting the environment and combating climate change is important to you, you may want to donate to an organization that maintains parks or plants trees.

These organizations exist to improve some aspect of society. You may want to support a shelter for unhoused people, a health organization working to cure cancer, or a local park that you love to visit. These nonprofit organizations need money for one simple reason: They don't make money, they spend money. And the money they spend often comes from donations. Many of those contributions come from supporters who make small donations, sometimes as little as a dollar.

And the way you give to a nonprofit can vary a lot. Donating money, of course, is one possibility. Or maybe you give your time after some kind of weather disaster, like a flood or hurricane, hits the area where you live. Maybe there's a toy drive in your area during the holidays, and you give away items you've outgrown.

Here's a real-life example: As a fourth-grade student, Dejuan Strickland, who goes by DJ, found himself without the money to buy lunch one day. "That really kind of stuck with me," DJ remembered later. It was not a feeling that he wanted other kids to experience. So, when DJ was fifteen, he started a GoFundMe with the goal of raising $200 to help parents at his former elementary school in his Missouri town pay for school lunches. In less than two weeks, he raised $400. Inspired to do more, he campaigned to raise more funds for his entire school district, which included more than thirty schools. And he met that goal. "Sometimes, school lunch is the only meal a kid can depend on," he wrote later. "Food insecurity is a huge issue, and I am doing what I can do to combat it."

Volunteering with a nonprofit can also offer you experience in an area you wouldn't get otherwise. Imagine that a girl named Luna wanted to help out after a tornado destroyed much of her hometown. Luna volunteered with the Red Cross, and she spent days keeping track of and distributing food, clothing, and building supplies to the people who had been hit the hardest. Along the way, she gained organizational skills as she helped get her town back on its feet.

Activity 10

With the help of an adult, find a nonprofit that means a lot to you. Maybe you want to help care for shelter animals. Does a food bank in your neighborhood need your help? If you have a particular interest in the environment, is there a nonprofit organization that is investing in clean energy options? There are many organizations out there! Find one that matches your interests and give back—either with your time or money.

Nonprofit organizations: groups created to serve a charitable need, rather than to make a profit to benefit their owners.

Philanthropy: the idea of giving money to people or organizations in need.

Donation: something given to a person or organization for no charge. A donation can be money, time, or a physical item.

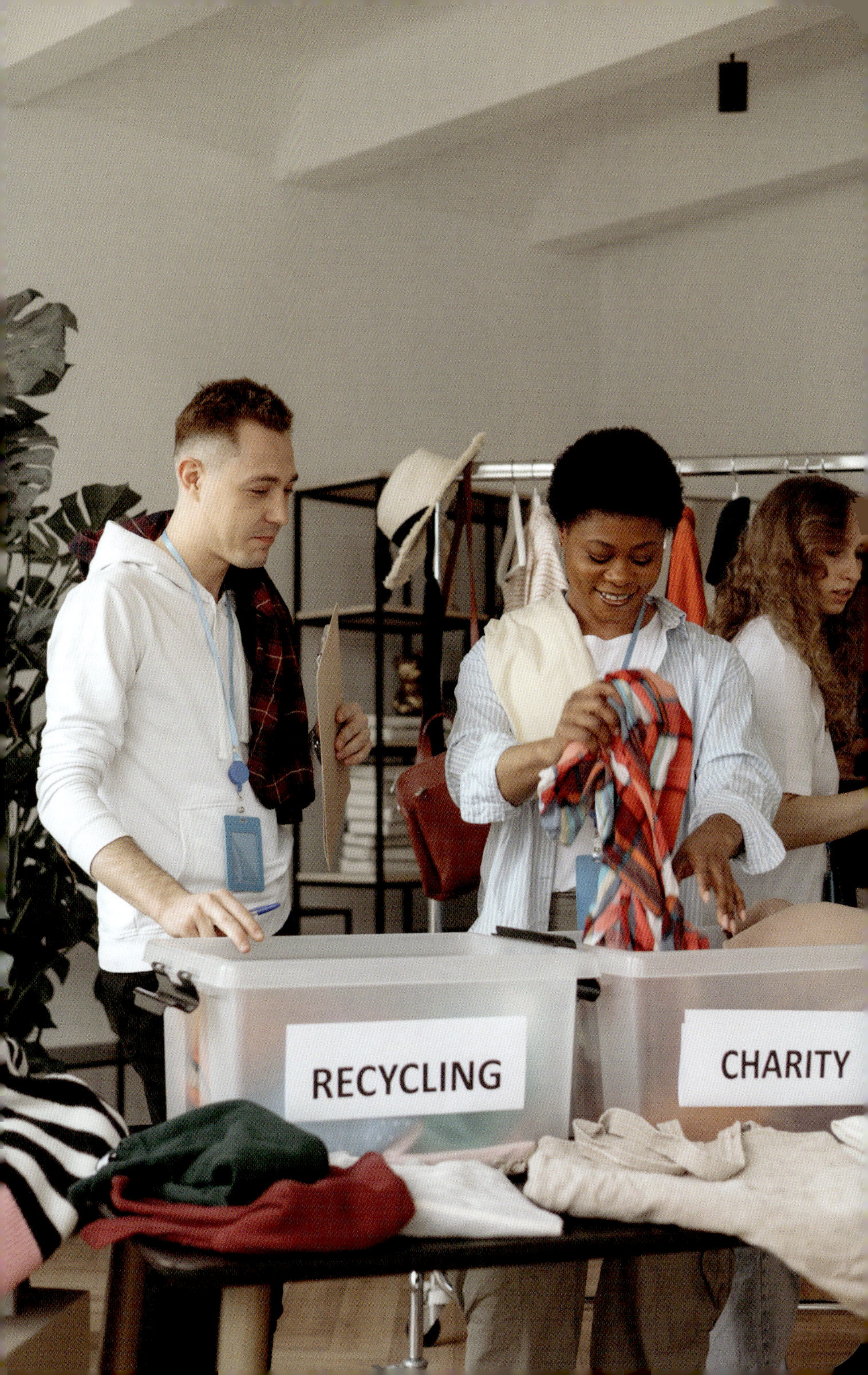
RECYCLING
CHARITY

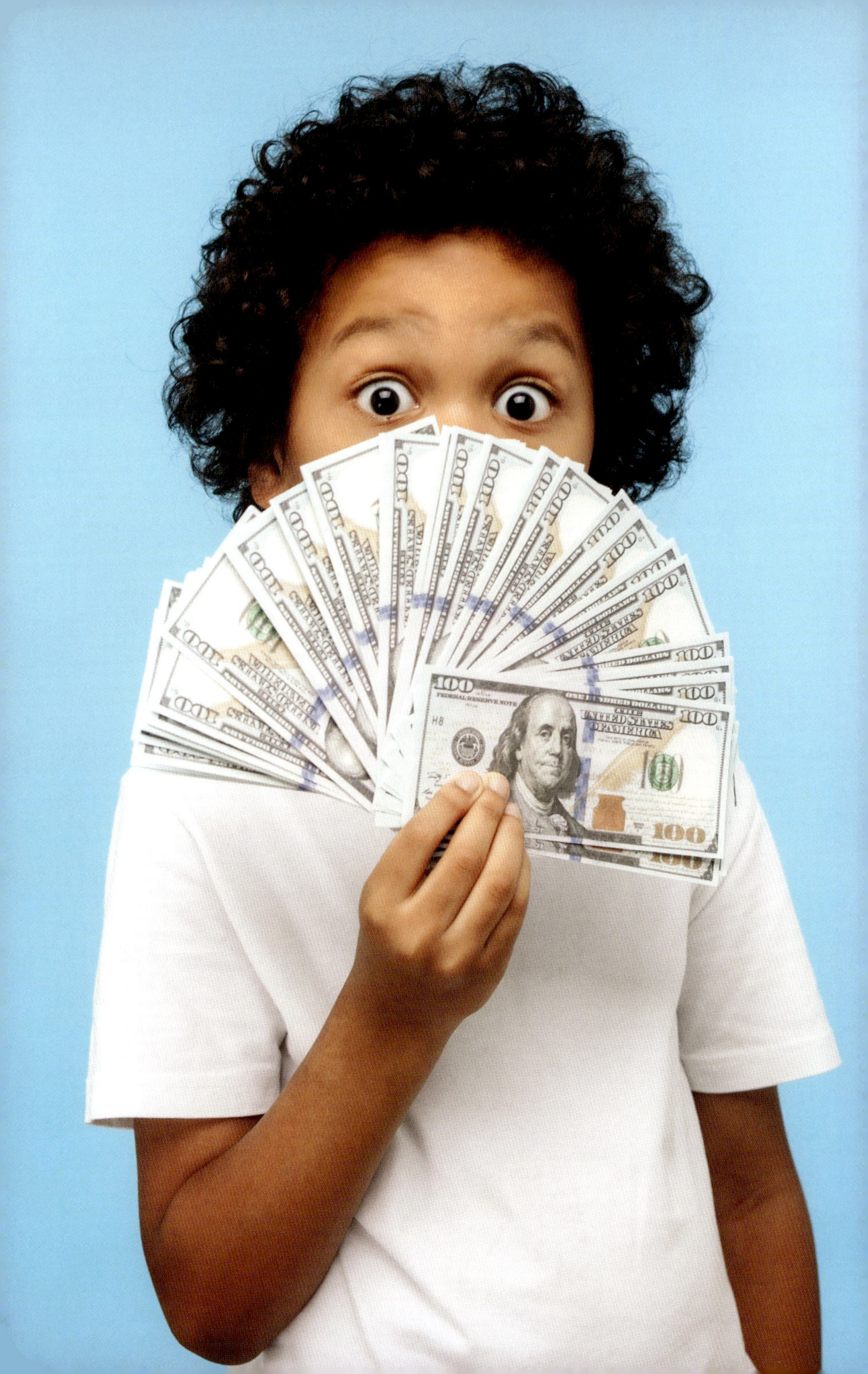
100
FEDERAL RESERVE NOTE
UNITED STATES OF AMERICA
100

CHAPTER 8
GO FORTH!

Clearly, when it comes to thinking about money, there's a lot to remember. New developments in the money space—like cryptocurrency—are bubbling up all the time, which means there's always even more to learn. Often, the way your money is earned, saved, and spent will depend as much on your feelings as it does on being logical about growing your bank accounts.

It's important to remember that what you do with your money is totally up to you, so think carefully about what you truly want. Do you want to invest? Do you want to save? Do you want to spend? The answers to these questions are not the same for everyone.

And don't let your age get in the way of thinking big. Imagine the case of Liza, who likes to make money shoveling snow but can only shovel one driveway at a time. But what if Liza organizes a group of kids who are all willing to shovel snow wherever she sends them? And what if she checks through her neighborhood for people who need the shoveling done and then connects the right kids with the right houses? Liza can earn a commission for each kid's work as well as continue to do her own shoveling, too.

Later on, as you get older and your experience grows, your opportunities to earn money will expand as well. The good news is that developing the right habits now will help you plan how to use money better in the future. When you're older, you will have bigger money decisions to make. You'll decide which job to take, whether to travel, and whether you want to buy a car or even a house. With good money habits firmly established, those decisions will be easier to make when the time comes.

And yet, although making money should be one of the cornerstones of your life, you want to keep it in its proper place. It may be better to earn less money at a job you love rather than earn more money at a job you don't really care for. Saving money is important, but it's more than okay to have a little fun along the way. Investing can be exciting, but too much excitement could end up costing you more than makes sense.

Always remember that money is only one piece of the jigsaw puzzle that makes you—your passions and your personality—who you are and what you will become. Money doesn't stand alone. As country singer Dolly Parton has wisely said, "Don't get so busy making a living that you forget to make a life."

Activity 11

Make a budget for yourself that covers an entire year. What do you think you spend on hobbies? Or snacks? Or entertainment? As the year progresses, is your spending actually matching up with what you planned for? If not, can you make adjustments from one category to another to keep you on course? Or do you have to cut back in order to avoid going into debt? Whatever your situation may be, the more you pay attention, the better the financial decisions you'll be able to make.

_____

_____

_____

_____